HELP! MY TEEN IS DEPRESSED

Christine Chappell

Consulting Editor: Dr. Paul Tautges

Help! My Teen Is Depressed

ISBN
Paper: 978-1-63342-204-9
epub: 978-1-63342-205-6
Kindle: 978-1-63342-206-3

Published by **Shepherd Press**
P.O. Box 24
Wapwallopen, PA 18660

www.shepherdpress.com

All Scripture quotations, unless stated otherwise, are from the ESV 2016.

Designed by **documen**

Contents

Introduction

My husband and I were thrust into our teen's battle with depression not long ago, and we've never felt more ill-equipped to respond. Though I myself have sailed the seas of sorrow many times in my teen and adult years, I never imagined my child would take such a journey. It broke my heart to discover she was walking down a road that I had traveled. I felt guilty, as if I could've done something to protect her from the melancholy. I felt regret, as if my history with depression had infected her emotional and physical composition.

Most of all, *I felt helpless*.

I wanted to fix her. I wanted our daughter to be the happy girl she used to be. But as time passed, we discovered the most important thing we could offer her was our faithful, compassionate presence—not our "fix-it-quick" promises.

You see, there are no quick and easy solutions

for healing your teen's depression. Chances are you're already beginning to sense this. You've tried strategies and remedies, but discouragement remains. Your child's moods shift from one day to the next. Conversations and arguments over medical care and counseling methods are taxing and tiresome. Perhaps you're slowly coming to the realization that you have no idea how to rescue your child from the darkness he or she is in.

You are not alone in your sense of helplessness and desperation. Many parents have found themselves frantically crying out to God, echoing the urgency of King Jehoshaphat's distress:

> *For we are powerless against this great horde that is coming against us. We do not know what to do, but our eyes are on you.*
> *(2 Chronicles 20:12)*

Yet, even as you diligently search for resources and support, there's something you need to remember: You are not the savior of your child's soul or the ultimate healer of his or her sorrow. Only God has the power to turn your child's darkness into light. He promises to lead you step by step as you continue to look to him for wisdom.

And I will lead the blind
in a way that they do not know,
in paths that they have not known
I will guide them.
I will turn the darkness before them
into light,
the rough places into level ground.
These are the things I do,
and I do not forsake them.

(Isaiah 42:16)

This verse isn't some hyperspiritual, feel-good pep talk, but a divine guarantee which finds its "Yes!" in Christ (2 Corinthians 1:20). If you've trusted in Jesus for the salvation of your soul, and have been born again by the Holy Spirit, you have the precise resources necessary to walk your child through depression in a way that honors God and blesses your child.

It's my hope that by reading this minibook, you'll gain practical biblical wisdom to help you care for your depressed teen. We'll explore the various ways God interacts with his despondent children, and learn how to apply these observations to your child's particular situation. In addition, you'll find comforts and cautions for your own heart. Caring for a depressed child will test you and tempt you to respond in sinful or harmful ways. Therefore, these pages are intended to offer hope for the hopeless teen and help for the helpless caregiver.

1 Understand the Experience of Depression

Author and biblical counselor Ed Welch writes,

> *There are times when depression is saying something and we must listen.*[1]

While it can be tempting to view your teen's depression as pouting, or simply the result of hormone fluctuations, the truth is that your child's despondency is an outward expression of internal unrest. Unbiblical assumptions about the nature of your child's depression can lead to unhelpful responses such as:

> *"What have you got to be sad about? You don't know how lucky you really are."*
> *"Toughen up and get over it already."*
> *"If you think positive thoughts, you'll start to feel better."*
> *"This is no way for a Christian to act."*
> *"Put on a happy face—fake it till you make it!"*

Perhaps you can identify with some of these statements. I know I can! I understand how tempting it can be to grow impatient with your teen's emotional instability. Oftentimes, in frustration, parents may resort to trite slogans and superficial encouragements. Even so, a "pull yourself up by your bootstraps" mentality is desperately insufficient to help our teens. In fact, any strategy that invites us to rely upon our own willpower for change is a limited resource at best, and painfully destructive at worst—

for not by might shall a man prevail.
(1 Samuel 2:9)

Before we get too far along, it's important to view depression through a biblical lens. When the Scriptures inform how you think about depression, your posture toward your teen can become more humble, gracious, and compassionate. Let's take a look at some core statements that offer a biblical framework for moving forward in your care.

Depression Is *Not* Abnormal

Understand that your teen's depression, though possibly severe, is not an abnormal human experience. It's ultimately the result of living in a fallen world that is broken by sin, death, mourning, crying, and pain (Revelation 21:4). Dr. Daniel Berger puts it succinctly:

> *If life in general is happy, then sadness should be viewed as an abnormality. But if life is generally sorrowful and fallen, then sorrow should be expected and understood—no matter how deep, enduring, or impairing—as a normal honest assessment of and reaction to life.*[2]

Think about it. Babies are born *crying*, not laughing. They need the warm, soothing embrace of someone else in order to find their calm. The same is true for us. To experience happiness, we need satisfaction, comfort, and pleasure that we cannot manufacture within ourselves. We constantly pursue happiness because it seems to elude us—no matter what we have, how much we have of it, or how long we have it for. This is why King Solomon, after reflecting on how much of his life was spent on empty pursuits and worldly priorities, concluded that

> *All is vanity.* (Ecclesiastes 1:14)

Pastor and author Timothy Keller explains,

> *Everybody knows that all parties are eventually going to be over—that all joy really does end in grief. . . . Death ends everything. Everything your heart wants out of life will eventually be taken away from you.*[3]

This is what is meant when Proverbs 14:13 observes,

> Even in laughter the heart may ache,
> and the end of joy may be grief.

Depression Is a Form of Suffering

It can be challenging to view your teen's depression as a form of suffering, but that is what it is. A biblical example is found in Psalm 88, which is often referred to as "the unresolved psalm." It is called this since, unlike the other songs in the book, this particular psalm does not end with any hope of resolution or rescue. Instead the writer honestly communicates his feelings of living in deep darkness, and reveals that we don't always get answers from God in the midst of our despair. Look at what the suffering writer says in this brief summary:

I am a man who has no strength . . .
like the slain that lie in the grave . . .
in the regions dark and deep . . .
my eye grows dim through sorrow . . .
Afflicted and close to death from my youth up,
I suffer your terrors; I am helpless. . . .
my companions have become darkness.
(*Psalm 88:4, 5, 6, 9, 15, 18*)

Psalm 88 is a peek into the heart of a believer in God who, despite his commendable faith, is suffering a season of unresolved, inexplicable sorrow. He finds himself physically isolated, spiritually wounded, and utterly unable to do anything about it except to lament over his pitiful condition. If this is the experience of a faithful man of God, how much more painful and confusing must depression be for a teenager with far less emotional and spiritual maturity?

If you personally have experienced depression in the past, remind yourself of its torture. If you have not experienced depression, try to put yourself in the shoes of the sufferer who penned Psalm 88. Your teen is feeling this unrest now, daily, hour by hour, minute by minute. Take the words of Charles Spurgeon to heart:

Yes, we would feel more for the prisoner if we knew more about the prison.[4]

Depression Involves *Both* Body and Soul

There are those who hold the view that depression is strictly a physical issue, and others who regard depression as solely spiritual. Many caregivers will come to the table with an opinion that depression is *either* physical *or* spiritual. However, if we believe our teen is depressed solely because of a spiritual issue, we may treat him or her with less compassion, or place blame upon him or her for this particular struggle. In similar fashion, if we believe depression is purely a physical issue, then we may ignore the necessity for evangelism and/or discipleship during the healing process.

The problem with these either/or approaches is that they're too simplistic, or reductionist. Humans are not merely biological organisms to manage through medication, nor are they merely spiritual beings impervious to the physical complications that arise from living in finite, fallen bodies. To better understand the dynamics at play we must first ground ourselves in a biblical understanding of the composition of man. Genesis 2:7 offers us a solid foundation:

> *then the* Lord *God formed the man of dust from the ground and breathed into his nostrils the breath of life, and the man became a living creature.*

In the very beginning, God created man as body and soul—both of equal value and necessity. God used dust from the ground (the physical component) as well as his own divine breath (the spiritual component) to bring Adam to life. Embracing this unity is imperative in our approach to helping our depressed teen. We need to consider possible physical components, and we need to recognize that our teen's spiritual care is important.

Does this mean depression always has a physical cause? No, not all depression finds its roots in an organic, physiological issue. Rather, because every human being is made in the image of God, and designed to live in relationship with him, there is always a spiritual component in the mix. So, while the treatment of depression may sometimes require more than soul care, it never requires less. Consider Proverbs 18:14:

> *A man's spirit will endure sickness,*
> *but a crushed spirit who can bear?*

A spirit that is well can persevere through bodily afflictions, but a crushed spirit cannot sustain a healthy body. That's why hopelessness is so dangerous. "The erosion of hope," Keller writes, "is what makes suffering unbearable."[5] While it may be true that your teen's body would benefit from medical care, a crushed spirit requires the kind of balm that only the living Word of God can supply:

> *For whatever was written in former days was written for our instruction, that through endurance and through the encouragement of the Scriptures we might have hope.*
>
> (Romans 15:4)

Depression Can Serve Redemptive Purposes

The truth that God can work good out of this season of depression (Romans 8:28) is a consolation to use sensitively. However, it's not without biblical merit to suggest that God intends to use this season of suffering to spiritually refine both you and your teen. Let's briefly consider three purposes.

First, you may find that your teen's depression serves as an opportunity for you to share the gospel with him or her. If your child has yet to place his or her hope in Christ, now is the time to extend God's gracious invitation. It may be God's plan that your teen comes to saving faith in Jesus because of this trial (Psalm 119:71). If your teen doesn't seem responsive to embracing the Lord Jesus Christ as Savior, pray and continue to gently teach him or her about Jesus when opportunities arise. Avoid "Bible bashing." Ask God for the power and ability to model the love of Christ to your child. Trust that he's working in your teen's heart to slowly reveal more and more of himself.

Second, this experience with depression may serve to draw you closer to your teen. Despondency is an opportunity for a rich discipleship relationship between caregiver and child. This is often an overlooked element of the healing process, but biblical one-another care is critical when tending to a crushed spirit. As a caregiver, you are tasked with offering compassionate encouragement and patient help.

> *And we urge you, brothers, admonish the idle, encourage the fainthearted, help the weak, be patient with them all.*
>
> (1 Thessalonians 5:14)

Third, one of the redemptive benefits of this painful situation is that God can use it to make you more like Jesus. You cannot always be sure of God's will in your teen's depression, but you can be certain that God desires for you to bear spiritual fruit as a result of it. To accomplish this, your child's struggle is going to expose areas of sin in your life. It's possible to become bitter when your teen doesn't show signs of improvement. You may become angry when you learn how little control you have over your child's enduring melancholy. However, this isn't only your child's journey—it's yours as well. As much as God is working in your child's heart, he insists on working in yours, too. Will you surrender and trust that he is training you in righteousness through this trial?

> *No discipline seems pleasant at the time,*
> *but painful. Later on, however, it produces*
> *a harvest of righteousness and peace for*
> *those who have been trained by it.*
>
> (Hebrews 12:11, NIV)

Perhaps you find yourself reading this minibook but you've yet to place your trust in Jesus Christ as Lord and Savior. I want you to know that the Lord is eager for you to know him as intimately as he knows you and your teen. God is a gracious Father who invites you to accept his free gift of eternal salvation through his only begotten Son:

> *I have swept away your sins like a cloud.*
> *I have scattered your offenses like the morning mist.*
> *Oh, return to me,*
> *for I have paid the price to set you free.*
> (Isaiah 44:22, NLT)

All of the biblical promises and comforts I share in this mini-book are freely available to you today through a personal relationship with Jesus Christ. Come to him now, confess your sin and your weariness, and feel the weight of the world lift off your shoulders as you cling to one of the most glorious promises God ever made:

> *I will be with you.* (Isaiah 43:2)

There are many ways you can (and probably will) sin as your teen walks the road of healing. It's necessary for you to remain mindful of your own weaknesses in the process (Matthew 7:5). You and your teen are in equal need of a Savior. You both are dependent upon God for all things. You don't understand everything that is going on with your teen's depression, and therefore you must trust God for the strength and wisdom needed to persevere in loving care.

> Trust in the Lord with all your heart,
> and do not lean on your own understanding.
> In all your ways acknowledge him,
> and he will make straight your paths.
> (Proverbs 3:5–6)

2 Observe God's Care

Do you see yourself as a minister of Christ in the midst of your teen's depression? Personally, I still feel the weightiness of this calling as I care for my daughter. Yet, despite feeling ill-equipped for the task, we're not left without a training manual: namely, the Bible. God's Word, in tandem with the power of the Holy Spirit, will supply the riches of grace we need in order to navigate these stormy seas. Charles Spurgeon once preached,

> *It is always well for ministers, and all who have the care of souls, to watch how God deals with those who are in trouble, just as a young surgeon, when he walks the hospital, is eager to see how a master in the healing art treats his patients.*[6]

In this chapter, we'll peer over the shoulder of God, the Great Physician, and observe how he treats his patients. We'll watch how the Lord deals with those who are crushed in spirit, and consider how to apply the same methods of care to your despondent teen.

Elijah's Death Wish

In the Old Testament book of 1 Kings, we find God's prophet, Elijah, at odds with his sworn enemy, Queen Jezebel. In response to hearing the report that Elijah had slaughtered 850 prophets of the false gods Baal and Asherah, Jezebel sent him a furious message: "You'll be dead by tomorrow" (see 1 Kings 19:1–2).

Elijah's fear of Jezebel's death threats immediately overtook his faculties. In despair, he retreated to the wilderness (19:3) and asked the Lord to take away his life:

> *And he asked that he might die, saying, "It is enough; now, O Lord, take away my life, for I am no better than my fathers."*
>
> (19:4)

How did God respond to Elijah's despair? He invited his exhausted prophet to rest (19:5). In his gracious providence, God gave Elijah a broom tree to lay his head under, offering just enough shade for two long, comfortable naps. An angel of the Lord was then summoned to touch Elijah with a hand of heavenly compassion. Cake was baked and water was fetched—twice—that Elijah might receive some long-overdue bodily nourishment (19:6).

When Elijah regained his physical strength, he took a long walk with his Maker to Horeb, the mountain of God. There, Elijah had honest conversations with the Lord about his fears and laments (19:10). God listened intently and asked questions (19:13). Through the physical and spiritual care of heaven, this fainthearted child of God was slowly nursed back to courageous faith, ready to receive his marching orders for the journey ahead of him (19:15).

God did not treat Elijah's physical condition as unimportant. In fact, God tended to the prophet's physical needs before tending to his spirit. And when the urgent bodily matters had been addressed, the Lord engaged Elijah in heart-probing conversation and faith-building fellowship. Notice, as we observe the Lord's care of Elijah, that we do not see rebukes or harsh treatment. Rather, we see that physical sustenance and gentle spiritual fellowship may sometimes be "just what the doctor ordered."

What does this mean for the care of your depressed teen?

1. *Take a Long, Hard Look at the Physical Condition of Your Child*

It can be easy to overlook things such as eating or exercise habits, water intake, sleep patterns, health history, recent bodily traumas, or pubescent changes. Is your teen burdened by excessive extracurricular commitments? Does his or her schedule leave no breathing room for rest and refreshment? If the Lord regarded factors like these as a critical element of Elijah's restoration, we too should pay careful attention to how our teen's body is (or isn't) being nourished and managed.

2. *It May Be Prudent to Schedule a General Physical Examination with Your Teen's Pediatrician*

While some seasons of depression can be the result of grief, abuse, trauma, or some life-changing form of loss or dashed hope, there are times when depression arrives unexpectedly—seemingly without any particular reason. In these cases, scheduling a checkup with your child's doctor for the purpose of ruling out any obvious physical issues is wise and fits well into the model we see here in the biblical narrative.

3. Patient Endurance and Gracious Fellowship with Your Teen Are Critical

It can be difficult to demonstrate love and compassion toward someone whose burden is so heavy. Your depressed teen may be prone to excessive grumbling, hypersensitivity, listlessness, withdrawal, crying fits, unprovoked outbursts, and the like. But just as God was patient with Elijah's despondent gripes, the Holy Spirit can empower you to extend grace to your child as you remember God's unmerited kindness and longsuffering toward you (Romans 5:8).

4. Don't Be in a Hurry to Get Your Child out of His or Her Sorrow

God could have restored the prophet at the snap of a finger—but he didn't. According to the biblical narrative, it took weeks for Elijah's darkness to be lifted. Understand that your teen's healing process is going to take the exact amount of time that God dictates is best (Isaiah 55:8–9). Because there are no quick fixes for despondent children, you must guard your heart against trading initial compassion for impatient bitterness. This journey will test your ability to love as humbly and faithfully as Christ has loved you (Ephesians 5:1–2). Remember that you are not called to "fix" your teen's depression, but you are called to love, encourage, and disciple him or her through it (1 Thessalonians 5:14).

Moses' Aggravated Complaint

In the book of Numbers, we read of another despairing request to die. When the relentless complaining of the Israelites finally broke Moses' spirit, he cried out to the Lord about the burden on his shoulders and begged to be spared the stress of managing the ungrateful nation by himself:

> *I am not able to carry all this people alone; the burden is too heavy for me. If you will treat me like this, kill me at once.*
>
> (Numbers 11:14–15)

In his aggravation, Moses waved a white flag of surrender before the Lord. Unable to understand how God expected him to endure such a stiff-necked people day in, day out, Moses wanted to give up on life itself. His bitter circumstances had effectively thrown Moses into a fit of hopeless unbelief. This narrative reiterates that real Christians can (and will, according to John 16:33) experience seasons in their lives when they are overwhelmed by perilous troubles. Consider Exodus 33:11:

> *the* Lord *used to speak to Moses face to face, as a man speaks to his friend.*

The very man that God called his "friend" had reached the end of his proverbial rope. Moses concluded that life wasn't worth living if such difficulty was going to remain. Even the deliverer of Israel—whom God had used to part the waters of the Red Sea—was capable of slipping into temporary hopelessness. As the well-known saying puts it, "The best of men are but men at best."

On this occasion, God's response didn't directly address a specific physiological or spiritual need. Although a rebuke certainly would have been warranted, the Lord provided crisis management help instead. Moses was told to gather seventy respected elders from the people in order to share the leadership burden (Numbers 11:16–17). God instructed Moses,

> *bring [the elders] to the tent of meeting . . . And I will come down and talk with you there.*

There are several important applications we can

derive by observing God's care of Moses' despair:

1. Sometimes Answers Are Hard to Come By

Your teen may be able to identify with the questions Moses voiced in the heat of the moment. *Why? Where? How? When?* Maybe you're asking yourself the same questions. This trial will often leave you face-to-face with confusion about God's involvement, and about what you're supposed to do to help your child. But God won't always offer clear explanations about the depression your teen is facing. Sometimes what seems like God's silence is actually an invitation for you to trust him and wait for him to work (Isaiah 55:8).

2. Your Teen Is Not Designed to Bear This Burden Alone

Just as God instructed Moses to surround himself with a group of respected, godly men (Numbers 11:16), so your teen needs the support of a community. For example, my family found tremendous relief in collaborating with our child's student-group leaders at church. By creating a plan for her to take small steps toward manageable social situations, we were able to support an eventual reintegration into the body of Christ for fellowship. Depression is an experience during which your child may feel unnoticed or estranged. Therefore making a concerted effort to rally a community around your child lets your child know that he or she is welcomed and important—that this depression is not your child's identity, nor does it determine his or her desirability in the body of Christ.

3. God Wants to Offer Your Teen Counsel and Consolation regarding His or Her Problems

It is one thing to have the loving support of a community, but your child also needs God's comfort and wisdom. God told Moses to bring the elders to the tent of meeting, and that he would discuss next steps with Moses once he did (Numbers 11:16–17). Depression offers your teen an opportunity to learn God's way to respond to life's hurts—a way that leads to life and settled assurance in the midst of suffering. Arrange for your child to be discipled by a biblical counselor or spiritual mentor, and God will do just as he did for Moses.

While there are many more stories that serve to demonstrate God's gracious, effective care of his sorrowing children, the accounts of Elijah's death wish and Moses' aggravated complaint are sufficient to acclimate your heart to a holistic, compassionate approach as you seek to care for your depressed teen. These biblical character studies help us to understand that depression affects both body and soul. They highlight the importance of community and biblical wisdom during the healing process. Most of all, they remind our weary hearts that the Lord sees our troubles, cares deeply about our pain, and intimately responds to the cries of his people.

> *Fear not, for I am with you;*
> *be not dismayed, for I am your God;*
> *I will strengthen you, I will help you,*
> *I will uphold you with my righteous right hand.*
>
> (Isaiah 41:10)

3

Get to the Heart

While it's impossible for you to know every physical and spiritual component at play in your teen's despondency, there are cues you can look for in his or her behaviors and words which can offer you discipleship opportunities. *Remember: your teen's depression is trying to say something* to you and others. The more intently you listen, engage, and invite his or her heart to speak, the more wisdom you can gain as you attempt to love and serve your teen well in the healing process. I'd like to help you narrow your focus onto the heart of your child.

> *The purpose in a man's heart is like deep water,*
> *but a man of understanding will draw it out.*
> (Proverbs 20:5)

To be caregivers "of understanding," as the proverb above suggests, we need to know how to draw out our teen's heart like water out of a deep well. Let's take a look at some of the common feelings associated with depression, and see how a closer examination can help us better minister to our teen in truth and love. The Personal Application Projects at the back of this mini-book also offer some helpful exercises for you to work through with your teen.

Fear

Think back over the past few weeks and ask yourself these questions: How often have you noticed your child appearing fearful or hesitant? Does your teen grow anxious in social situations? Is he or she scared to go to school? Experiencing separation anxiety? Worrying excessively about the family's financial situation? Suffocated by a loathsome dread of death? Afraid that past traumas will recur? Panicked by a sudden change of plans? Terrified something bad is about to happen?

Your teen's fearful behaviors and anxiety-ridden statements expose his or her heart's spiritual allegiance. While it's true that there are many frightening experiences we must face in this life, fears become disordered when they impede our ability to function. Our hearts cannot help but grow fearful when we place our trust in people or possessions rather than in our faithful God.

Your teen's depression may serve to expose false securities he or she's been clinging to in order to make sense of the overwhelming feelings within and the broken world around.

Getting to the heart of our teen's fearful disposition means asking about what (or whom) our teen is trusting in when he or she grows frightened or panicked. Listen patiently. Affirm you hear what your teen is saying. Avoid phrases like, "You don't need to be worried about that." Instead, acknowledge your teen's experience and use the opportunity to share the comfort that God soothes fearful people with: the promise of his presence:

> *the* LORD *. . . goes before you. He will be with you; he will not leave you or forsake you. Do not fear or be dismayed.*
>
> (Deuteronomy 31:8)

Anger

Do you feel like you're walking on eggshells around your teen? Does he or she seem easily irritated and quick to argue? Do seemingly minor annoyances snowball into unmanageable frustrations? If you have observed a steady increase in your teen's anger levels as he or she has waded through the muck of depression, you're on to something important:

Sadness + Anger = Depression.[7]

Teens, like us, are prone to believe that the world should revolve around their wants and needs. Because the Scriptures tell us that unrighteous anger stems from self-centered desires at war within our hearts (James 4:1), we need to help our teens closely examine their anger with some self-reflection questions:[8]

- What are my personal needs? "Needs" is usually a euphemism for "rights" and "demands."
- Where have my needs been unmet?
- Where have my rights been violated?
- What do I think I deserve that I haven't received?
- Of whom am I jealous?

Oftentimes, anger results from a desire to judge and punish others for perceived injustices. It's possible your teen may be harboring resentment toward someone believed to have wronged him or her—*God included.*

Even if our child's anger is a valid, righteous reaction to an actual transgression that has occurred, we need to help our teen understand that God can be relied upon to exercise justice on his or her behalf (Romans 12:19). Keep in mind: addressing anger issues is best handled when everyone involved comes to the table with a calm and humble spirit—don't attempt it during a fit of rage! Refer to the Personal Application Projects for additional guidance on overcoming anger by grace.

Identity

The teen years usher in a period of confusion related to matters of identity. Whether our teens are struggling with issues related to sex, gender, academics, athletics, or the scars of past traumas and abuse, instability in their identity stabs at the very core of their being. Identity refers to the primary lens through which they view themselves.

Depression provides an occasion for identity issues to show. Is your teen crushed in spirit because a recent injury has stolen his or her ability to play sports? Does your teen pressure him- or herself toward academic perfection? Does your teen seem to absorb the mannerisms and fashion preferences of his or her ever-changing social circles? Has an important relationship become fractured recently?

While the issue of identity may not have entered your mind as a possible component of your child's depression, its implications cannot be ignored if you are going to help your child to think biblically. False conclusions concerning one's identity can manifest themselves in a variety of ways, but here are a few of the common ones:

- Perfectionism: I must meet certain standards to be worthy of love and acceptance.
- Guilt: I've done something wrong and there's no fixing it.
- Shame: I've done something wrong—or someone has done something wrong to me—and everyone knows about it.
- Loneliness: I'm all alone—no one understands or cares.

How each of these points may work into your teen's experience of depression is going to be unique, and by no means is this an exhaustive study on the topic of biblical identity. However, opening your eyes to the fact that these concerns may be at work in the heart of your despondent child is important. Caregivers need to become reflexive in offering the message of gospel hope and help to children grappling with temptations to adopt an identity of their own making. We can do this by turning to the Scriptures and talking about God's design for mankind; the perfect life, sufficient death, and victorious resurrection of Jesus Christ; and how faith in God's Son makes us a new creation here on earth and heirs to the promise of everlasting life in heaven.

> *But you are a chosen race, a royal priesthood, a holy nation, a people for his own possession, that you may proclaim the excellencies of him who called you out of darkness into his marvelous light.*
>
> (1 Peter 2:9)

Grief and Loss

Your teen's depression may be linked to recent grief or loss. Though death may have been involved, grief can stem from the loss of anything that was loved, valued, or treasured. Maybe your child had his or her hopes set on something important to him or her, but it fell through, and your child is grieving the loss of that particular unfulfilled good desire. It's normal to be sad when we lose someone or something we have great affection for. We experience grief when God gives us something good and then, in his providence, takes it away from us (Job 1:21).

When your depressed teen is navigating feelings of grief and loss, it's important to follow the apostle Paul's instruction to

> *weep with those who weep.*
>
> *(Romans 12:15)*

Your teen's sorrow can make you uncomfortable, and as a result, you may be tempted to be insensitive with your responses. A trite slogan will gloss over your teen's grief as unnecessary, pointing to God's sovereignty to minimize his or her heartbreak. An impatient rebuke of your teen's grief will hurry him or her to move past it, insisting that because life goes on, your teen should just "get over it." But whatever the cause of hurt, your teen requires sympathy and comfort—not haste or insensitivity. Imitate the care of the Lord as he draws near to the brokenhearted to bind up their wounds (Psalm 34:18).

Some common causes of grief and loss are:

- » The death of a loved one.
- » A change in neighborhoods or schools.
- » The relocation of friends and family.
- » Sudden and/or significant physical impairment/injury.
- » Loss of innocence through physical/sexual abuse.
- » Divorce or parental separation.

Each of these can open the door to your teen possibly sinking deeply toward hopelessness. Be mindful: there are no quick fixes. Work in tandem with the Holy Spirit to do the slow and steady work of restoring hope for the future. Your child's story may be tragically sad now, but in Christ, the story isn't finished. The Author of your teen's story is also the Author of life, and with him is plentiful redemption (Psalm 130:7). Jesus assures us that sadness and tears will be wiped away (Revelation 21:4). But, until then, all of us must find glimpses of hope for tomorrow by placing our trust in God today.

Your teen's depression may be complicated. While I can't present every potential heart issue in this mini-book, I hope that I've given you a good start to peeling back the layers. If your child is working with a biblical counselor or mentor, you should explore how you can partner with that person. Remember, in his wisdom, God specifically chose you to be the parent of your child. Together with a mature believer, you can gain further insights into the various feelings, thoughts, and desires that may be compounding your teen's experience of depression. It's also important to remember that paying attention to spiritual issues is only one facet of a biblically holistic approach, which remains mindful of potential physical influences as well.

4 Prepare for Common Challenges

Depression can vary in degree of severity. No two people will experience it in the same way. However, there are challenges specific to your teen's stage of life that it is important for you to be mindful of. This chapter unpacks some common challenges.

Considering Medication

The issue of whether or not your child might benefit from taking prescription medication for the symptoms associated with his or her depression is a discussion that needs to take place between you, your teen, and a reliable physician. Although there's no one-size-fits-all approach to the issue of medication for the treatment of depression symptoms, there are important considerations when carefully weighing the options. You might also want to consult one or two of the resources listed in the "Where Can I Get More Help?" section at the end of this mini-book.

While major depressive disorder is one of the most common mental disorders in children and adolescents, studies reveal the use of pharmacological interventions in this population is still a matter of controversy.[9] The US National Library of Medicine published findings in a 2016 study indicating that fourteen commonly prescribed antidepressant drugs "do not seem to offer a clear advantage for children and adolescents" when considering the overall risks and benefits.[10]

Here are some additional points to consider when thinking through a plan to help your teen:

1. Antidepressants Carry Significant Risks That Are Specific to Children

It's not uncommon for some children to experience worsening symptoms as a result of taking antidepressants. Many prescription labels warn of increased suicidal ideations in the children who take them. If your child's darkness already includes suicidal thinking, medication may actually serve to inflame those dangerous urges and thought patterns.[11]

2. Psychiatric Prescriptions Attempt to Manage Symptoms, Not Treat Causes

While we call antidepressants "medications," they don't facilitate internal physical healing. Their intent is to lessen some of the symptoms experienced during depression. It's wise to approach antidepressants as an aspirin that may (although, not always, and not without risks) serve to alleviate symptoms without treating the depression's underlying cause.[12]

3. Don't Let Your Child Have Access to the Medication

Some depressed teens struggle with suicidal thoughts, so easy access to pills can serve as an irresistible temptation to attempt an overdose. Keep medications locked away, give them at regularly scheduled times, and ensure they are being swallowed. Skipping doses can be dangerous once your teen's body has adjusted to the prescription's presence in his or her system.

If you do decide to permit your teen to take a psychiatric prescription, it's important to have an honest conversation with him or her about the dangers, the potential for it to do more harm than good, and the necessity of communicating with you right away about any side effects he or she notices. For further direction about best practices for medication management, consult your child's doctor.

When Hospitalization Becomes Necessary

Not every teen who battles depression will struggle with self-harm or suicidal urges, but there may be occasions when their physical safety will require hospitalization. If your teen has communicated that he or she has recently had thoughts of hurting him- or herself or other people, urgent attention is required.

What might it look like for your teen to go to the hospital in this situation? Admit your teen to the local emergency room, where the medical staff can perform routine evaluations such as blood work and brain scans, and perform a risk evaluation on your child. The ER staff will want to rule out any obvious physical conditions which may be contributing to your teen's acute distress.

If the medical tests come back clear, the attending physician will discuss options for safety and possibly recommend your teen be admitted to a pediatric behavioral hospital for further observation and evaluation. If your teen is admitted to a behavioral/mental hospital, you can expect the duration of the stay to last anywhere from three to seven days, on average, depending on state requirements and the particulars of your child's case.

If a trip to the psychiatric hospital becomes part of your family's story, it doesn't mean you have failed your child. Many other families have gone through this heartbreaking process. It's understandable to be upset and to lament over the desperation of the situation. *Remember: there is no building or institution that keeps God's presence away from your child* (Psalm 139:7). Trust Jesus to care for your teen while he or she is hospitalized, make an effort to see your teen as often as possible during visitation hours, and pray without ceasing while he or she is away from home.

Issues at School

Teens who are depressed may also struggle at school. While some children are able to keep up their academic performance, others may find that their inability to focus becomes so severe that simply sitting at a desk for hours a day requires a monumental effort.

You may not understand why it's so challenging for your child to buckle down and get his or her work done, but adding to your teen's sense of inadequacy during this season of healing is harmful. Depressed teens have a negative "ticker tape" playing nonstop in their minds, constantly accusing them of being weak, a failure, or a burden to everyone around them. Assume he or she is already self-condemning with regards to school performance.

The truth is, it will be hard for your teen to perform well in school while he or she is despondent. Your teen may experience memory issues, distracting anxiety, waves of sudden panic, a sense of disassociation, and a general lethargy while in an academic setting. Perhaps his or her sleeping and eating habits are erratic. If your child is taking a prescription, side effects could also be impacting his or her ability to learn.

Pray to avoid the temptation of being harsh toward your teen because of the difficulty he or she is having. Assure your child that you'll help to construct a reasonable plan which makes accommodations for these cognitive challenges. Meet with the school counselor and find out what options are available to help support your child. Affirm your child and let him or her know that your love is not dependent upon academic performance. Encourage your teen to focus on the day's work and tasks, instead of worrying about how to rebound from these setbacks in the future.

> *Therefore do not be anxious about tomorrow, for tomorrow will be anxious for itself. Sufficient for the day is its own trouble.*
>
> (*Matthew 6:34*)

Friends and Social Life

Depression is a time when isolation reigns. Your teen may feel uncomfortable being around his or her peers. Friends may ask, "What's wrong?" and your child will be uneasy about answering them honestly. He or she may feel quickly overwhelmed by social stimulus and long for the stillness of solitude. Because his or her thoughts are often so harassing, external chaos only serves to stoke the fires of internal turmoil.

You may also discover that your teen's social life is actually a contributing factor in his or her depression. Perhaps he or she is being bullied at school. Maybe a relationship turned sour and your teen is feeling rejected. Whatever the case may be, your child may crave seclusion while wrestling with confusing internal angst.

Caregivers play a lot of parts when it comes to caring for a depressed teen, and the role of *friend* is an important one. While friends may seem few and far between, you have the opportunity to offer a ministry of friendly presence to your child.

Make time to step into your teen's world. Watch a movie. Play a game. Read the Scriptures aloud together. Toss a ball. Try some coloring sheets or easy creative art projects. Ask if there is a particular activity he or she would like to do with you. Go on a scenic drive. Sit in his or her bedroom, listen to music, or watch a favorite show.

Behavioral Concerns

Your teen's depression does require gracious accommodations, but it does not excuse sinful words or deeds on his or her part. Be careful when correcting your child's emotional volatility. If you're quick to anger and slow to listen when your child becomes upset, you'll discipline him or her out of impatience instead of wisdom (James 1:19–20). Guard your heart against answering your teen's sin with your own:

> *Brothers, if anyone is caught in any transgression, you who are spiritual should*

restore him in a spirit of gentleness. Keep watch on yourself, lest you too be tempted.
(Galatians 6:1)

So how can you give grace to your child when it comes to discipline issues in his or her depression? Remember that your teen is hurting—the pain of the suffering amplifies his or her emotional sensitivity to minor grievances. Your teen is dealing with confusing emotions and physical stressors, and isn't equipped to respond in a fruitful way. While the physical weaknesses that often accompany depression cannot *make* your teen sin, they do offer an occasion for your child's heart to stumble. Use these times to teach your teen about the lavish forgiveness that is available through confession and repentance (1 John 1:9).

Think about it: How often do *you* fall short in obeying God when difficulties come? Jesus Christ is the only person who was tempted while he suffered and yet never sinned (Hebrews 4:15)! Identify with your teen as a fellow sinner in need of grace. Thanks be to God that there is forgiveness in Christ for the times our responses to life's challenges fall horribly short of righteous (Romans 7:21–25).

Is his or her behavior blatantly defiant? If so,

discipline is warranted. Talk with your teen up front about how correction will be handled during this season. It's true that your child needs an extra amount of grace during this trial—but grace is not license for the total disregard of parental authority (Romans 6:1–2).

> *Good sense makes one slow to anger,*
> *and it is his glory to overlook an offense.*
> *(Proverbs 19:11)*

Is the behavior a minor offense worthy to be overlooked or gently corrected in love? Grumbling, complaining, or a general attitude of negativity may serve as an opportunity to engage your teen in conversation instead of discipline. Listen closely and collect data about the inner wars being waged in your teen's heart.

You may also find your teen walking a fine line between genuine struggle and manipulating parents. If your teen is constantly using the experience of depression as an excuse to avoid activities or situations he or she simply doesn't like, a firm pushback may be appropriate. Consulting with your teen's counselor can help you discern whether or not manipulation is taking place.

Pray for wisdom—does your teen require your

comfort or your challenge in this moment? Be careful not to punish sadness, crying, worry, fear, failure, and panic; these things aren't defiance, but responses to grief, pain, confusion, and hopelessness. Remember that, above all, your teen needs to be assured of your love and the love of God for him or her despite the depression (1 John 4:10).

Conclusion

As you continue on this journey with your depressed teen, you might be tempted to make your child's healing an ultimate goal instead of a desired goal. *Beware: it's possible to idolize the eradication of your teen's depression.* If this happens, you'll place an impossible urgency upon your child's shoulders. If he or she isn't "cured"—and quickly—you'll run the risk of growing angry and bitter about it. If you don't end up blaming your child for his or her despondency, you'll accuse God for his apparent failure to help get rid of it.

Idolizing healing will only end in frustration, and possibly even a fractured relationship between you and your teen. Your teen cannot "fix" him- or herself through a formula any more than you could "fix" yourself through obedience to God's law.

I'd like to leave you with a few parting words of encouragement, some dos and don'ts as you continue to explore additional resources and find support for your teen's healing process.

- *Don't carry the weight of your child's depression alone.* Involve your pastor or a biblical counselor or mentor throughout the whole journey. You need to bring another person into your child's life, someone to speak to other than you. He or she needs that outlet, and you need help shouldering the burden. See the "Where Can I Get More Help?" section at the end of this mini-book for helpful websites.
- *Do constantly remind your child of your love.* Sometimes you won't have the right words to say. But a heartfelt "I love you" is never misplaced or ill-timed. When you don't know what to say, grab hold of your child tightly and remind him or her that your child is deeply loved, no matter what.
- *Don't have unreasonable expectations for the healing process.* Depression is often cyclical in nature. It ebbs and flows. Your child may take two steps forward and three steps back. The road ahead is long—there's no formula that guarantees a swift eradication of the despondency. Pray for your endurance, for your child's perseverance, and that the experience as a whole will bring you closer to

your teen and to the Lord.

» *Do constantly point to the humanity of Christ.* We cannot walk everywhere our child goes in life, but there is One who is like your child, who knows what it is to wrestle with the darkness of this world. In Christ, your teen has a friend who can identify with his or her pain and sympathize in ways we cannot. Remind your child that Christ has endured what he or she is going through, and has lived to tell about it! Jesus has promised to be with your teen always, and especially in the midst of despondency. These truths are a great source of comfort and hope.

» *Don't see your depressed teen as a "problem" to be solved.* Life is busy, and when your teen endures a prolonged battle against depression, it's tempting to begin to view him or her as a problem to solve instead of a child to love. Guard your heart against this temptation by remembering the long-suffering of God toward you. Resist the urge to grow frustrated because the depression has not lifted yet. Do what you know you have been called by God to do: love him, and love your teen as yourself (Mark 12:30–31).

» *Do pray without ceasing and resolve to wait on the Lord.* Your teen needs your prayers. Depression is a season when spiritual warfare is at its most fierce. Intercede for your child, knowing God hears you and is at work in the situation (John 5:17). Confess to the Lord when you find yourself wavering in resolve. While you cannot know all of the ways God intends to redeem your teen's depression, you can be certain that, in part, the trial is meant to humble, test, and teach *you*. Many of the truths you preach to your teen will be reminders for your weary heart as well.

» *Do seek to grow in areas of your life that God reveals along the way.* Hard circumstances serve to reveal soft spots in your faith. While you can't know all the ways God is working through this situation, you can be sure he wants to use your teen's struggles to teach *you* to walk more faithfully in the ways of Jesus (1 Thessalonians 3:4).

God has equipped you for this hard calling. When he knit this child together in the womb, he knew depression would be part of his or her story. The Lord placed the two of you together for a very specific, good, and fruitful purpose. Through this trial, you'll come to lean upon the Lord's wisdom, grace, and strength in ways you never knew were possible. Your teen will learn about the Father of mercies and the God of all comfort (2 Corinthians 1:3), who alone has the power to restore his or her crushed spirit and weary body. Together, you'll walk side by side, and learn that the faith that weeps while it waits is not weak. It is not the strength of our faith, but the object—Jesus Christ—that gives us the hope necessary to endure this challenging season.

As you seek to honor God through your care, you'll begin to sense his presence more keenly in the everyday moments between you and your son or daughter. In the arguments and in the tears, he is there. In the slammed doors and the late night sobs, he is there. In the counseling appointments and the car rides home, he is there. With every victorious step forward and painful slide back, take heart and don't give up on your child. You've wept and you've prayed—Christ has heard and is near (Isaiah 43:2–3).

Personal Application Projects

This section offers exercises that can serve as discipleship tools. Your teen may require help in thinking through these reflections, so be sure to create unhurried, quiet time where you can work through the projects together.

1. Equip your child with the language of biblical lament by reviewing Psalms 10:1; 22:1; 88:14; 89:46; and 90:13. Ask your son or daughter which of these laments he or she can identify with, and to explain why. Cry out together in a prayer of lament to God, or have your child write out a personal lament, modeled after the pattern seen in the Scriptures.

2. Help your child explore his or her fits of rage or frustration.[13] Talk about a recent situation that tempted your child to become angry, and work through the following five biblical truths which help us overcome anger by grace. Invite your child into surrender, confession, and repentance afterwards.

- » I get angry when I want something too much (James 4:1–2).
- » I am not God or a judge (Genesis 50:19; Romans 12:17–21).
- » God has been very gracious to me; therefore I can be gracious with others (Ephesians 4:31–32; Matthew 18:21–35).
- » God is in control, and I can trust him (Genesis 50:20; Romans 8:28; 1 Corinthians 10:13).
- » Christ made me a new creation—I can now choose to respond in grace instead of anger (Romans 6:11; 2 Corinthians 5:17).

3. Give your teen a pack of blank note cards and a book of stamps. Task your teen with writing and mailing a note of encouragement to a friend or family member. Our teens need help getting their focus off of themselves, and even small acts of kindness toward others is an excellent way to help them do so.

4. Find a service activity you can do as a family that would interest your teen. Some ideas are volunteering at a soup kitchen, elderly care facility, animal shelter, and so on. If you can

connect an interest of your teen's to a volunteer opportunity, it can offer him or her a sense of purpose and bring refreshment to your teen's spirits through serving (Isaiah 58:10–11).

5. Grab a plastic bag and take your teen for a walk, collecting interesting-looking natural materials (leaves, sticks, flowers, bark, rocks, etc.) as you stroll. Talk about the things you collect and place in the bag. What makes them remarkable? Where did they come from? What do they feel like? Count the different types of birds you see. How many different animals do you pass? Observing creation and getting fresh air is needful and refreshing for your teen's body and soul. Take a moment to pray with your teen, giving thanks to God for the creativity and beauty of his creation.

6. Encourage your child to be a functioning member of the family by establishing a clear expectation for chore assignments. Agree on a reasonable and regular schedule for household tasks and hold your teen accountable for completing them.

Where Can I Get More Help?

Resources for Medicine/Psychiatric Concerns

Berger II, Daniel R., *Rethinking Depression: Not a Sickness, Not a Sin* (Taylors, SC: Alethia International Ministries, 2019).

Emlet, Michael R., *Descriptions and Prescriptions: A Biblical Perspective on Psychiatric Diagnoses and Medications* (Greensboro, NC: New Growth Press, 2017).

Hodges, M.D., Charles D., *Good Mood, Bad Mood: Hope and Help for Depression and Bipolar Disorder* (Wapwallopen, PA: Shepherd Press, 2013).

Welch, Edward T., *Depression: A Stubborn Darkness* (Greensboro, NC: New Growth Press, 2004).

Other Helpful Books

Bridges, Jerry, *Trusting God: Even When Life Hurts* (Colorado Springs, CO: NavPress, 1988).

Cole, Cameron, *Therefore I Have Hope: 12 Truths That Comfort, Sustain, and Redeem in Tragedy* (Wheaton, IL: Crossway, 2018).

Eswine, Zack, *Spurgeon's Sorrows: Realistic Hope for Those Who Suffer from Depression* (Fearn, Ross-shire: Christian Focus, 2014).

Priolo, Lou, *Keeping Your Cool: A Teen's Survival Guide* (Phillipsburg, NJ: P&R, 2014).

Somerville, Bob, *If I Am a Christian, Why Am I Depressed?* (Maitland, FL: Xulon Press, 2014).

Tautges, Paul, *A Small Book for the Hurting Heart: Meditations on Loss, Grief, and Healing* (Greensboro, NC: New Growth Press, 2020).

Vroegop, Mark, *Dark Clouds, Deep Mercy: Discovering the Grace of Lament* (Wheaton, IL: Crossway, 2019).

Welch, Edward T., *Side by Side: Walking with Others in Wisdom and Love* (Wheaton, IL: Crossway, 2015).

LifeLine Mini-Books

Keeter, Tim, *Help! My Child Is Being Bullied* (Wapwallopen, PA: Shepherd Press, 2019).

Newheiser, Jim, *Help! My Anger Is Out of Control* (Wapwallopen, PA: Shepherd Press, 2015).

Ray, Bruce, *Help! My Friend Is Suicidal* (Wapwallopen, PA: Shepherd Press, 2016).

Trahan, Carol, *Help! I'm Depressed* (Wapwallopen, PA: Shepherd Press, 2014).

Online Resources

Locate a certified biblical counselor in your community at biblicalcounseling.com/counselor.

For free biblical resources on depression and related issues, visit ibcd.org/resources.

To better equip yourself to offer one-another care for your teen and others, visit ibcd.org/cdc.

For biblical conversations about life's challenging problems, stream the *Hope & Help* podcast at christinemchappell.com.

For biblical curricula pertaining to emotions, anxiety, psychiatric disorders, shame and guilt, loss, addictions, and more, visit ccef.org/curriculum.

Endnotes

1 Edward T Welch, *Depression: A Stubborn Darkness* (Greensboro, NC: New Growth Press, 2004), 32.

2 Daniel R Berger II, *Rethinking Depression: Not a Sickness, Not a Sin* (Taylors, SC: Alethia International Ministries, 2019), 31.

3 Timothy Keller, "The Wounded Spirit," Redeemer Presbyterian Church, December 5, 2004, https://gospelinlifecom/downloads/the-wounded-spirit-5388/, accessed October 23, 2019.

4 Charles Spurgeon, "A Troubled Prayer," Sermon 741, Classic Christian Library, http://classicchristianlibrarycom/library/spurgeon_charles/Spurgeon-Metropolitan-pt13pdf, accessed October 22, 2019.

5 Timothy Keller, *Walking with God Through Pain and Suffering* (New York: Penguin, 2016), 313.

6 Charles Spurgeon, *The Silent Shades of Sorrow: Healing for the Wounded* (Fearn, Ross-shire: Christian Heritage, 2015), 83.

7 Welch, *Depression*, 153.

8 Ibid, 155.

9 A Cipriani et al, "Comparative Efficacy and Tolerability of Antidepressants for Major Depressive Disorder in Children and Adolescents: A Network Meta-Analysis," US National Library of Medicine, National Institutes of Health, https://www.ncbi.nlm.nih.gov/pubmed/27289172, accessed November 7, 2019.

10 Ibid.

11 US Food & Drug Administration, "Suicidality in Children and Adolescents Being Treated with Antidepressant Medications," https://www.fda.gov/drugs/postmarket-drug-safety-information-patients-and-providers/suicidality-children-and-adolescents-being-treated-antidepressant-medications, accessed November 7, 2019.

12 Welch, *Depression*, 211.

13 Jim Newheiser, "Anger Mismanagement," Institute for Biblical Counseling and Discipleship, 2012, https://ibcd.org/anger-mismanagement/, accessed October 30, 2019.

BOOKS IN THE HELP! SERIES INCLUDE...

- Help! He's Struggling with Pornography
- Help! Someone I Love Has Been Abused
- Help! My Toddler Rules the House
- Help! Someone I Love Has Cancer
- Help! I Want to Change
- Help! My Spouse Has Been Unfaithful
- Help! Someone I Love Has Alzheimer's
- Help! I Have Breast Cancer
- Help! I'm a Slave to Food
- Help! My Teen Struggles With Same-Sex Attractions
- Help! She's Struggling With Pornography
- Help! I Can't Get Motivated
- Help! I'm a Single Mom
- Help! I'm Confused About Dating
- Help! I'm In a Painful Marriage
- Help! I'm Drowning in Debt
- Help! My Teen is Rebellious
- Help! I'm Depressed
- Help! I'm Living With Terminal Illness
- Help! I Feel Ashamed
- Help! I Want to Model Submission in Marriage
- Help! I Can't Handle All These Trials
- Help! I Can't Forgive
- Help! My Anger is Out of Control
- Help! My Friend is Suicidal
- Help! I'm in a Conflict
- Help! I'm Being Deployed
- Help! I've Been Traumatized by Combat
- Help! I'm So Lonely
- Help! My Kids Are Viewing Pornography
- Help! I Need a Church
- Help! I'm Anxious
- Help! My Parents Abused Me When I was a Kid

More titles in preparation

For current listing go to: www.shepherdpress.com/lifeline

About Shepherd Press Publications

- » They are gospel driven.
- » They are heart focused.
- » They are life changing.

Our Invitation to You

We passionately believe that what we are publishing can be of benefit to you, your family, your friends, and your work colleagues. So we are inviting you to join our online mailing list so that we may reach out to you with news about our latest and forthcoming publications, and with special offers.

Visit:

www.shepherdpress.com/newsletter

and provide your name and email address.